D1496334

The Essential P. K. Page

The Essential P. K. Page

selected by Arlene Lampert
and Théa Gray

The Porcupine's Quill

Library and Archives Canada Cataloguing in Publication

Page, P.K. (Patricia Kathleen), 1916 –
[Poems. Selections]
   The essential P.K. Page / selected by Arlene Lampert and Théa Gray.

(Essential poets ; 2)
Poems.
ISBN 978-0-88984-308-0

   I. Lampert, Arlene, 1934 –   II. Gray, Théa   III. Title.
IV. Series: Essential poets (Erin, Ont.) 2

PS8531.A34A6 2008   C811'.54   C2008-904586-6

Published by The Porcupine's Quill, 68 Main Street, P.O. Box 160,
Erin, Ontario N O B I T O. www.sentex.net / ˜pql

Represented in Canada by the Literary Press Group.
Trade orders are available from University of Toronto Press.

We acknowledge the support of the Ontario Arts Council and the Canada
Council for the Arts for our publishing program. The financial support of the
Government of Canada through the Book Publishing Industry Development
Program is also gratefully acknowledged. Thanks, also, to the Government
of Ontario through the Ontario Media Development Corporation's Ontario
Book Initiative.

Table of Contents

7   Foreword

9   Address at Simon Fraser (excerpt)
10 After Rain
12 After Reading *Albino Pheasants* by Patrick Lane
14 Ah, by the Golden Lilies
16 Ancestors (from *Melanie's Nite-Book*)
17 And about Death
18 Another Space
20 Arras
22 As on a Dark Charger
23 A Backwards Journey
24 Beside You
25 Custodian
26 Deaf-Mute in the Pear Tree
28 Dwelling Place
28 Ecology
29 Evening Dance of the Grey Flies
30 The Filled Pen
31 Funeral Mass
32 A Grave Illness
33 Hand Luggage (excerpts)
34 The Hidden Room
35 Hughes
36 Inebriate
37 Intraocular Lens Model 103G
38 Leather Jacket
39 Like a Cruise Ship
40 Macumba: Brazil
42 Man with One Small Hand
43 The Mole
43 Motel Pool
44 The New Bicycle
45 On Educating the Natives
45 Picking Daffodils
46 Poem Canzonic with love to AMK

48 Remembering

49 The Selves

50 soft travellers

52 Stargazer

52 Stefan

53 Stories of Snow

55 Suddenly

56 This Heavy Craft

56 This Sky

57 Traveller's Palm

58 Truce

58 Winter Morning

58 The World

59 Young Girls

60 Zero Is Zero (from *Alphabetical*)

Foreword

The poetry of P.K. Page needs no introduction, although a note on the format may be helpful.

P.K. Page is a poet who writes in many genres and on an infinite number of subjects and has done so all her writing life. In reading her work it is impossible to distinguish the early poems from the later. There is not a 'young' voice and a 'mature' voice. For her, time is not linear and she places little value on such distinctions. For this reason we have decided to arrange the poems alphabetically for easy reference.

We think of this small volume as a sort of pocket P.K. Page and hope it will make its way into backpacks, carry-on luggage and doctors' waiting rooms.

We dedicate this selection to the poet who wrote it.

– Arlene Lampert and *Théa Gray*

Address at Simon Fraser (excerpt)

If we'll but give it time, a work of art
'can rap and knock and enter in our souls'
and re-align us – all our molecules –
to make us whole again. A work of art,
could, 'had we but world enough and time,'
portray for us – all Paradise apart–
'the face (we) had/before the world was made,'
or, to compound the image, vivify
Plato's invisible reality.

But is there time enough? This turning world
we call our home, or *notre pays* – could
become inimical to humankind –
humanunkind as cummings might have said –
in fewer years than I have walked this earth.

So, what is there to tell you? Only this.
'Imagination is the star in man.'
Read *woman*, if you wish. And though we are
trapped in the body of an animal,
we're half angelic, and our angel ear,
which hears the music of the spheres, can hear
the planet's message, dark, admonishing,
as the archaic torso of Apollo
admonished Rilke, 'You must change your life.'

Art and the planet tell us. Change your life.

After Rain

The snails have made a garden of green lace:
broderie anglaise from the cabbages,
Chantilly from the choux-fleurs, tiny veils –
I see already that I lift the blind
upon a woman's wardrobe of the mind.

Such female whimsy floats about me like
a kind of tulle, a flimsy mesh,
while feet in gumboots pace the rectangles –
garden abstracted, geometry awash –
an unknown theorem argued in green ink,
dropped in the bath.
Euclid in glorious chlorophyll, half drunk.

I none too sober slipping in the mud
where rigged with guys of rain
the clothes-reel gauche
as the rangy skeleton of some
gaunt delicate spidery mute
is pitched as if
listening;
while hung from one thin rib
a silver web –
its infant, skeletal, diminutive,
now sagged with sequins, pulled ellipsoid,
glistening.

I suffer shame in all these images.
The garden is primeval, Giovanni
in soggy denim squelches by my hub,
over his ruin
shakes a doleful head.
But he so beautiful and diademed,
his long Italian hands so wrung with rain
I find his ache exists beyond my rim
and almost weep to see a broken man
made subject to my whim.

O choir him, birds, and let him come to rest
within this beauty as one rests in love,
till pears upon the bough
encrusted with
small snails as pale as pearls
hang golden in
a heart that knows tears are a part of love.

And choir me too to keep my heart a size
larger than seeing, unseduced by each
bright glimpse of beauty striking like a bell,
so that the whole may toll,
its meaning shine
clear of the myriad images that still –
do what I will – encumber its pure line.

After Reading *Albino Pheasants* by Patrick Lane

Pale beak … pale eye … the dark imagination
flares like magnesium. Add but *pale flesh*
and I am lifted to a weightless world:
watered cerulean, chrome-yellow (light)
and green, veronese – if I remember – a soft wash
recalls a summer evening sky.

At Barra de Navidad we watched the sky
fade softly like a bruise. Was it imagination
that showed us Venus phosphorescent in a wash
of air and ozone? – a phosphorescence flesh
wears like a mantle in bright moonlight,
a natural skin-tone in that other world.

Why should I wish to escape this world?
Why should three phrases alter the colour of the sky
the clarity, texture even, of the light?
What is there about the irrepressible imagination
that the adjective *pale* modifying *beak, eye* and *flesh*
can set my sensibilities awash?

If with my thickest brush I were to lay a wash
of thinnest watercolour I could make a world
as unlike my own dense flesh
as the high-noon midsummer sky;
but it would not catch at my imagination
or change the waves or particles of light

yet *pale* can tip the scales, make light
this heavy planet. If I were to wash
everything I own in mercury, would imagination
run rampant in that suddenly silver world –
free me from gravity, set me floating sky-
ward – thistledown – permanently disburdened of my flesh?

Like cygnets hatched by ducks, our minds and flesh
are imprinted early – what to me is light
may be dark to one born under a sunny sky.
And however cool the water my truth won't wash
without shrinking except in its own world
which is one part matter, nine parts imagination.

I fear flesh which blocks imagination,
the light of reason which constricts the world.
Pale beak … pale eye … pale flesh … My sky's awash.

Ah, by the Golden Lilies

... ah, by the golden lilies,
the tepid, golden water,
the yellow butterflies
over the yellow roses ...

— *Yellow Spring,* Juan Ramón Jiménez

Jiménez, but for the roses
you paint a Rio garden
where every golden morning
the golden sunlight spills
on my Brazilian breakfast –
coffee like bitter aloes
strawberry-fleshed papayas
the sensuous persimmon ...
My young head full of follies
ah, by the golden lilies.

Beneath the cassia boughs
where fallen yellow blossoms
reflect a mirror image
I barefoot in the petals
trample a yellow world
while small canaries flutter
over the lotus pond.
I trail my golden fingers –
for I am Midas' daughter –
in the tepid, golden water.

My blue and gold macaw
laughs his demented laughter
dilates his golden pupils –
a golden spider spins
a spangled golden web
for beauty-loving flies.
Above the cassia branches –
the cassia coloured sun.
Above the yellow lilies –
the yellow butterflies.

Jiménez, I am freed
by all this golden clangour.
Jiménez, your roses
denote a falling sound
a sound that will not rhyme
with *sambas jocosos*
macumba, feijoada
Bahían *vatapá.*
A different sun disposes
over the yellow roses.

Ancestors

(from *Melanie's Nite-Book*)

The cavernous theatre filled with them,
going back
generation on generation,
dressed in the colours of power:
scarlet and purple and black,
plumed and surpliced and gowned.
Men with arrogant Roman faces,
women like thoroughbred horses
held in check.

These were the people for whom
I had lived in exemplary fashion,
had not let down,
for whom I'd refrained from evil,
borne pain with grace.
And now they were here – resurrected –
the damned demanding dead,
jamming a theatre like head-cheese,
smelling of mothballs and scent,
brilliantine, shoe polish, Brasso
and old brocade.

Row after row
and tier after tier they ranged,
crowded together like eels
in the orchestra pit,
squeezed in the quilted boxes
and blocking the aisles
while I, on the stage alone,
last of the line,
pinned by the nails of their eyes,
was expected to give an account.

But the gypsies came in the nick
and flung themselves about.
They stamped their naked feet
dark with the dust of Spain,
clattered their castanets,
rattled their tambourines,
brandished their flashing knives
and put the lot to rout.

And about Death

1.
And at the moment of death
what is correct procedure?

Cut the umbilical, they said.

And with the umbilical cut
how then prepare the body?

Wash it in sacred water.
Dress it in silk for the wedding.

2.
I wash and iron for you
your final clothes
(my heart on your sleeve)
wishing to wash your flesh
wishing to close
your sightless eyes

nothing remains to do

I am a vacant house

Another Space

Those people in a circle on the sand
are dark against its gold
turn like a wheel
revolving in a horizontal plane
whose axis – do I dream it? –
vertical
invisible
immeasurably tall
rotates a starry spool.

Yet *if* I dream
why in the name of heaven are fixed parts
within me set in motion
like a poem?

Those people in a circle reel me in.
Down the whole length of golden beach I come
willingly pulled by their rotation
slow
as a moon pulls waters
on a string
their turning circle winds around its rim.

I see them there in three dimensions yet
their height implies another space
their clothes'
surprising chiaroscuro postulates
a different spectrum.
What kaleidoscope
does air construct
that all their movements make a compass rose
surging and altering?
I speculate
on some dimension I can barely guess.

Nearer I see them dark-skinned.
They are dark. And beautiful.
Great human sunflowers spinning in a ring
cosmic as any bumble-top
the vast
procession of the planets in their dance.
And nearer still I see them – 'a Chagall' –
each fiddling on an instrument – its strings
of some black woollen fibre
and its bow – feathered –
an arrow almost.
                        Arrow *is*.

For now the headman – one step forward shoots
(or does he bow or does he lift a kite
up and over the bright pale dunes of air?)
to strike the absolute centre of my skull
my absolute centre somehow
with such skill
such staggering lightness
that the blow is love.

And something in me melts.
It is as if a glass partition melts –
or something I had always thought was glass –
some pane that halved my heart
is proved, in its melting, ice.

And to-fro all the atoms pass
in bright osmosis
hitherto
in stasis locked
where now a new
direction opens like an eye.

Arras

Consider a new habit – classical,
and trees espaliered on the wall like candelabra.
How still upon that lawn our sandalled feet.

But a peacock rattling its rattan tail and screaming
has found a point of entry. Through whose eye
did it insinuate in furled disguise
to shake its jewels and silk upon that grass?

The peaches hang like lanterns. No one joins
those figures on the arras.
                              Who am I
or who am I become that walking here
I am observer, other, Gemini,
starred for a green garden of cinema?

I ask, what did they deal me in this pack?
The cards, all suits, are royal when I look.
My fingers slipping on a monarch's face
twitch and go slack.
I want a hand to clutch, a heart to crack.

No one is moving now, the stillness is
infinite. If I should make a break ...
take to my springy heels ...? But nothing moves.
The spinning world is stuck upon its poles,
the stillness points a bone at me. I fear
the future on this arras.
                              I confess:

It was my eye.
Voluptuous it came.
Its head the ferrule and its lovely tail
folded so sweetly; it was strangely slim
to fit the retina. And then it shook

and was a peacock – living patina,
eye-bright – maculate!
Does no one care?

I thought their hands might hold me if I spoke.
I dreamed the bite of fingers in my flesh,
their poke smashed by an image, but they stand
as if within a treacle, motionless,
folding slow eyes on nothing. While they stare
another line has trolled the encircling air,
another bird assumes its furled disguise.

As on a Dark Charger

As on a dark charger
the night wind arrives,
brushing the thick, cold laurel leaves
and the slim willow knives.
        The night is opulent, larger
        to greet the young wind
        riding his dark charger.
But the wild swallows
and martins are pinned
like paper copies of birds
to the protecting eaves
above the slim willow knives
and laurel leaves.
        As, on a dark charger,
        insolent, rich,
        rides the young wind
        over the land.
        A new-peeled switch
        in his bare hand.
        Onward he swings,
        grows larger and larger,
        whistles and sings
        as on a dark charger.

A Backwards Journey

When I was a child of say, seven,
I still had serious attention to give
to everyday objects. The Dutch Cleanser –
which was the kind my mother bought –
in those days came in a round container
of yellow cardboard around which ran
the very busy Dutch Cleanser woman
her face hidden behind her bonnet
holding a yellow Dutch Cleanser can
on which a smaller Dutch Cleanser woman
was holding a smaller Dutch Cleanser can
on which a minute Dutch Cleanser woman
held an imagined Dutch Cleanser can ...

This was no game. The woman led me
backwards through the eye of the mind
until she was the smallest point
my thought could hold to. And at that moment
I think I knew that if no one called
and nothing broke the delicate jet
of my attention, that tiny image
could smash the atom of space and time.

Beside You

1.
I lay beside you
soft and white as dough
put by to rise

I rose and rose and rose

2.
We sounded *e*
above high *c*
the note
broke all my crystal
in a flash
smashed your plate glass

3.
My body flowers
in blossoms
that will fall
petal by petal
all the days of my life

Custodian

I watch it.
Lock and stock.
No joke.
It is my job.

I dust, I wash, I guard
this fading fibre;
polish even.
Spit.

And rub I it
and shine
and wear it to the bone.
Lay bare its nub.

It is but matter
and it matters not
one whit or tittle
if I wear it out.

Yet mend I it and darn
and patch
and pat it even
like a dog

that which the Auctioneer
when I am gone,
for nearly nought
will knock down
from his block.

Deaf-Mute in the Pear Tree

His clumsy body is a golden fruit
pendulous in the pear tree

Blunt fingers among the multitudinous buds

Adriatic blue the sky above and through
the forking twigs

Sun ruddying tree's trunk, his trunk
his massive head thick-knobbed with burnished curls
tight-clenched in bud

(Painting by Generalić. Primitive.)

I watch him prune with silent secateurs

Boots in the crotch of branches shift their weight
heavily as oxen in a stall

Hear small inarticulate mews from his locked mouth
a kitten in a box

Pear clippings fall
                    soundlessly on the ground
Spring finches sing
                    soundlessly in the leaves

A stone. A stone in ears and on his tongue

Through palm and fingertip he knows the tree's
quick springtime pulse

Smells in its sap the sweet incipient pears

Pale sunlight's choppy water glistens on
his mutely snipping blades

and flags and scraps of blue
above him make regatta of the day

But when he sees his wife's foreshortened shape
sudden and silent in the grass below
uptilt its face to him

then air is kisses, kisses

stone dissolves

his locked throat finds a little door

and through it feathered joy
flies screaming like a jay

Dwelling Place

This habitation – bones and flesh and skin –
where I reside, proceeds through sun and rain
a mobile home with windows and a door
and pistons plunging, like a soft machine.

Conforming as a bus, its 'metal' is
more sensitive than chrome or brass. It knows
a pebble in its shoe or heat or cold.
I scrutinize it through some aperture

that gives me godsview – see it twist and change.
It sleeps, it weeps, its poor heart breaks,
it dances like a bear, it laughs, opines
(and therefore *is*). It has a leafy smell

of being young in all the halls of heaven.
It serves a term in anterooms of hell,
greying and losing lustre. It is dull.
A lifeless empty skin. I plot its course

and watch it as it moves – a house, a bus;
I, its inhabitant, indweller – eye
to that tiny chink where two worlds meet –
or – if you so discern it – two divide.

Ecology

If a boy
eats an apple
because a bee
collects nectar,
what happens
because a boy
eats an apple?

Evening Dance of the Grey Flies

Grey flies, fragile, slender-winged and slender-legged
scribble a pencilled script across the sunlit lawn.

As grass and leaves grow black
the grey flies gleam –
their cursive flight a gold calligraphy.

It is the light that gilds their frail
bodies, makes them fat and bright as bees –
reflected or refracted light –

as once my fist
burnished by some beam I could not see
glowed like gold mail and conjured Charlemagne

as once your face
grey with illness and with age –
a silverpoint against the pillow's white –

shone suddenly like the sun
before you died.

The Filled Pen

Eager to draw again,
find space in that small room
for my drawing-board and inks
and the huge revolving world
the delicate nib releases.

I have only to fill my pen
and the shifting gears begin:
flywheel and cogwheel start
their small-toothed interlock

and whatever machinery draws
is drawing through my fingers
and the shapes that I have drawn
gaze up into my eyes.
We stare each other down.

Light of late afternoon –
white wine across my paper –
the subject I would draw.
Light of the stars and sun.

Light of the swan-white moon.
The blazing light of trees.
And the rarely glimpsed bright face
behind the apparency of things.

Funeral Mass

In his blackest suit
the father carries the coffin

It is light as a box of kleenex
He carries it in one hand

It is white and gold
A jewel box

Their baby is in it

In the unconscionable weather
the father sweats and weeps

The mother leans
on the arms of two women friends

By the sacred light of the church
they are pale as gristle

The priests talk Latin
change their elaborate clothes

their mitres, copes
their stoles embroidered by nuns

Impervious to grief
their sole intention

is the intricate ritual
of returning a soul to God

this sinless homunculus
this tiny seed

A Grave Illness

Someone was shovelling gravel all that week.
The flowering plums came out.
Rose-coloured streets
branched in my head –
spokes of a static wheel
spinning and whirring only when I coughed.
And sometimes, afterwards, I couldn't tell
if I had coughed or he had shovelled. Which.

Someone was shovelling until it hurt.
The rasp of metal on cement, the scrape
and fall
of all that broken rock.
Such industry day after day. For what?
My cough's accompanist?
The flowering trees
blossomed behind my eyes in drifts of red
delicate petals. I was hot.
The shovel grated in my breaking chest.

Someone was shovelling gravel. Was it I?
Burying me in shifts and shards of rock
up to my gasping throat. My head was out
dismembered, sunken-eyed
as John the Baptist's on a plate.
Meanwhile the plum
blossoms trickling from above
through unresistant air
fell on my eyes and hair
as crimson as my blood.

Hand Luggage (excerpt one)

Calgary. The twenties. Cold and the sweet
melt of chinooks. A musical weather.
World rippling and running. World
watery with flutes. And woodwinds.
The wonder of water in that icy world.
The magic of melt. And the grief of it. Tears –
heart's hurt? heart's help?

Hand Luggage (excerpt two)

Though sickness and death take their terrible toll
and they did and they do – one's astonishing heart
almost sings through its grief like a bird – water bird –
in the wind and the waves of some vast salty sea.
Explain it? I can't. But it's true I'm in love
with some point beyond sight, with some singular star
for which words won't suffice, which reduce it, in fact.
Head on it's invisible, if I should look
with my cones, not my rods,[1] it would vanish – expunged;
if I glance to the side, through my rods, then the star
shines as brightly as Venus. Which truth is *the* Truth?

*

Nero fiddled. And fiddled. What else could he do?

---

1 Cones and rods are the light-sensitive photoreceptors of the retina.

The Hidden Room

I have been coming here since I was born
never at my will
only when it permits me

Like the Bodleian like the Web
like Borges' aleph
it embodies all

It is in a house
deeply hidden in my head
It is mine and notmine

yet if I seek it
it recedes
down corridors of ether

Each single version
is like and unlike
all the others

a hidden place
in cellar or attic
matrix of evil and good

a room
disguised as a non-room
a secret space

I am showing it to you
fearful you may not
guess its importance

that you will see only
a lumber room
a child's bolt-hole

Will not know it as prism
a magic square
the number nine

Hughes

He spoke to the diamond in me
and the ruby.
And I saw a man rise
from the hidden black waters
of under-earth – spangled
a godman – drenched
and writing prism
on a sheet of glass.

Through his poems he taught me scale
and intensity
and he taught me that beauty
such as we see –
is the lowest note
in an infinite scale.
And he taught me dazzle.

Dazzled, I said
You're a genius, Ted.
It's not me, he said.

Inebriate

During the day I laugh and during the night I sleep.
My favourite cooks prepare my meals,
my body cleans and repairs itself,
and all my work goes well.

> – I Have Not Lingered in European Monasteries,
> Leonard Cohen

Here is eternity as we dream it – perfect.
Another dimension. Here the ship of state
has sprung no leaks, the captain doesn't lie.
The days are perfect and each perfect minute
extends itself forever at my wish.
Unending sunlight falls upon the steep
slope of the hillside where the children play.
And I am beautiful. I know my worth
and when I smile I show my perfect teeth.
During the day I laugh and during the night I sleep.

A dreamless, healing sleep. I waken
to everlasting Greece as white and blue
as music in my head –
an innocent music.
I had forgotten such innocence exists,
forgotten how it feels
to live with neither calendars nor clocks.
I had forgotten how to un-me myself.
Now, as I practise how and my psyche heals,
my favourite cooks prepare my meals.

I am not without appetite, nor am I greedy.
My needs are as undemanding as my tastes:
spring water, olives, cucumber and figs
and a small fish on a white plate.
To lift my heart I have no wish for wine –
the sparkling air is my aperitif.
Like Emily I am inebriate.
Rude health is mine – and privilege. I bathe
in sacred waters of the river Alph.
My body cleans and repairs itself.

Poised between Earth and Heaven, here I stand
proportions perfect – arms and legs outspread
within a circle – Leonardo's man.
So do I see the giddy Cosmos. Stars
beyond stars unfold for me and shine.
My telephoto lens makes visible
time future and time past, and timeless time
receives me like its child. I am become
as intricate and simple as a cell
and all my work goes well.

Intraocular Lens Model 103G

This lens I look through is as clear as glass.
It shows me all I saw before was false.

If what *was* true is true no longer, how
now can I know the false true from true true?

Leather Jacket

One day the King laid hold on one of the peacocks
and gave orders that he should be sewn up in a leather jacket.

– Suhrawardi

That peacock a prisoner
that many-eyed bird
blind.

Enclosed in a huge leather purse.
Locked in darkness.
All its pupils sealed
its tiny brain sealed
its light and fluttering heart
heavy as a plum.

Its life vegetable.
That beautiful colourful bird
a root vegetable.

Cry, cry for the peacock
hidden in heavy leather
sewn up in heavy leather
in the garden

among flowers
and flowering trees
near streams
and flowering fountains
among cicadas
and singing birds.

The peacock sees nothing
smells nothing
hears nothing at all
remembers nothing

but a terrible yearning
a hurt beyond bearing
an almost memory
of a fan of feathers
a growing garden

and sunshine falling
as light as pollen.

Like a Cruise Ship

It is like a cruise ship bursting into flower
or a municipal building intricately blooming.
And its myriad miniature petals blink as I pass.

Each year it grows more outrageous, spreads itself
unpruned, untended, a vegetable amphitheatre
with pizzicato blossoms pinking the air.

Oh, tree! I say as I whizz past, bowing. I bow. I whizz
powered by some high-octane fumeless fuel
that spring has invented. Oh, tree! I say. *Tree. Tree!*

And the word is new – *another* of spring's inventions.
Newer than *biots* or *quarks* or *nanoseconds.*

Macumba: Brazil

they are cleaning the chandeliers
they are waxing the marble floors
they are rubbing the golden faucets
they are burnishing brazen doors
they are polishing forks in the *copa*
they are praising the silver trays

their jerkins are striped like hornets
their eyes are like black wax

they are changing the salt in the cupboards
they are cooking *feijão* in the kitchen
they are cutting tropical flowers
they are buying herbs at the market
they are stealing a white rooster
they are bargaining for a goat

they are dressed in white for macumba
their eyes are like black coals

they are making a doll of wax
they are sticking her full of pins
they are dancing to the drums
they are bathed in the blood of the rooster
they are lighting the beach with candles
they are wading into the ocean
with presents for Iamanjá

they are dressed in the salt of the ocean
their eyes are like bright flames

they are giving her gifts of flowers
they are throwing her tubes of lipstick
they are offering shoes and scarves
brassieres and sanitary napkins
whatever a woman needs
they are flinging themselves on the waters
and singing to Iamanjá

they are drenched and white for macumba
and their eyes are doused and out

Man with One Small Hand

One hand is smaller than the other. It
must always be loved a little like a child;
requires attention constantly, implies
it needs his frequent glance to nurture it.

He holds it sometimes with the larger one
as adults lead a child across a street.
Finding it his and suddenly alien
rallies his interest and his sympathy.

Sometimes you come upon him unawares
just quietly staring at it where it lies
as mute and somehow perfect as a flower.

But no. It is not perfect. He admits
it has its faults: it is not strong or quick.
At night it vanishes to reappear
in dreams full-size, lost or surrealist.

Yet has its place like memory or a dog –
is never completely out of mind – a rod
to measure all uncertainties against.

Perhaps he loves it too much, sets too much stock
simply in its existence. Ah, but look!
It has its magic. See how it will fit
so sweetly, sweetly in the infant's glove.

The Mole

The mole goes down the slow dark personal passage –
a haberdasher's sample of wet velvet moving
on fine feet through an earth that only
the gardener and the excavator know.

The mole is a specialist and truly
opens his own doors; digs as he needs them
his tubular alleyways; and all his hills
are mountains left behind him.

Motel Pool

The plump good-natured children play in the blue pool:
roll and plop; plop and roll;

slide and tumble, oiled, in the slippery sun
silent as otters, turning over and in,

churning the water; or – seamstresses – cut and sew
with jackknives its satins invisibly.

Not beautiful, but suddenly limned with light
their elliptical wet flesh in a flash reflects it

and it greens the green grass, greens the hanging leaf
greens Adam and Eden, greens little Eve.

The New Bicycle

All the molecules in the house
readjust on its arrival,
make way for its shining presence
its bright dials,
and after it has settled
and the light
has explored its surfaces
– and the night –
they compose themselves again
in another order.

One senses the change at once
without knowing what one senses.
Has somebody cleaned the windows
used different soap
or is there a bowl of flowers
on the mantelpiece? –
for the air makes another shape
it is thinner or denser,
a new design
is invisibly stamped upon it.

How we all adapt ourselves
to the bicycle
aglow in the furnace room,
turquoise where turquoise
has never before been seen,
its chrome gleaming
on gears and pedals,
its spokes glistening.
Lightly resting on the incised
rubber of its airy tires
it has changed us all.

On Educating the Natives

They who can from palm leaves and from grasses
weave baskets of so intricate a beauty
and simply as a girl combing her hair,
are taught in a square room by a square woman
to cross-stitch on checked gingham.

Picking Daffodils

They have spilled their slippery juices over me
let fall saliva from their long green stems
Their viscous threads of water swing into my house
remind me of the waters of your mouth

Poem Canzonic with love to A M K

The sky is prussian blue, no, indigo
with just the merest hint of *ultramar*.
I am not painting it, so what care I?
And yet, I do care, deeply, as if life
depended on my skill to mix that blue.
Not my life only – your life, damn it! – *our*
whole planetary life:
the life of beetle, and ichneumon fly
plankton, crustacean, elk and polar bear
the delicate veined leaf
that blows against an enigmatic sky.

It is the writer's duty to describe
freely, exactly. Nothing less will do.
Just as the painter must, from two make three
or conjure light, build pigments layer on layer
to form an artefact, so I must probe
with measuring mind and eye to mix a blue
mainly composed of air.
What is my purpose? This I cannot say
unless, that I may somehow, anyhow
chronicle and compare
each least nuance and inconsistency.

This is the poem Abraham Moses Klein
wrote better, earlier, so why should I
write it again in this so difficult form?
His was a *tour de force*, a *cri de coeur*.
Mine is an urgent need to recombine
pigments and words, and so to rectify
and possibly restore
some lost arcanum from my past, some Om
secure, I thought, until I lost the key
or it lost me; before
birth intervened and – like a chloroform –

erased my archive, made me start again.
Vestigial memory only – vaguest dream
looming through mists, or like St. Elmo's fire
high in the riggings and phantasmal masts,
my one-eyed guide to seeing further in
or further out, to up-or-down the stream
of unremembered pasts –
might show me how to mix and how to name
that blue that is not cobalt or sapphire,
or fugitive, or fast;
and find the key that opens Here – and There.

Remembering

Remembering you and reviewing
our structural love
the past re-arises alive
from its smothering dust.

For memory, which is only decadent
in hands like a miser's
loving the thing for its thingness,
or in the eyes of collectors who assess
the size, the incredible size, of their collection,
can, in the living head, create and make
new the sometimes appallingly ancient present
and sting the sleeping thing
to a sudden seeing.

And as a tree with all its leaves relaxed
can shiver at the memory of wind
or the still waters of a pool recall
their springing origin and rise and fall
suddenly over the encircling basin's lip –
so I, remembering from now to then,
can know and see and feel again, as jewels
must when held in a brilliant branch of sun.

The Selves

Every other day I am an invalid.
Lie back among the pillows and white sheets
lackadaisical O lackadaisical.
Brush my hair out like a silver fan.
Allow myself to be wheeled into the sun.
Calves'-foot jelly, a mid-morning glass of port,
these I accept and rare azaleas in pots.

The nurses humour me. They call me 'dear'.
I am pilled and pillowed into another sphere
and there my illness rules us like a queen,
is absolute monarch, wears a giddy crown
and I, its humble servant at all times, am its least
serf on occasion and excluded from the feast.

Every other *other* day I am as fit
as planets circling.
I brush my hair into a golden sun,
strike roses from a bush,
rare plants in pots
blossom within the green of my eyes, I am
enviable O I am enviable.

Somewhere in between the two, a third
wishes to speak, cannot make itself heard,
stands unmoving, mute, invisible,
a bolt of lightning in its naked hand.

soft travellers

some words can make you weep,
when they're uttered, the light rap of their
destinations, their thud as if on peace, as if on cloth,
on air, they break all places intended and known

         – Inventory, Dionne Brand

there is magic, of course, and among the many magics there are
words – spell-binders, but there is also sleight-of-hand,
and the magic of herbs, which perhaps a shaman
knows for healing, words
do not necessarily heal, they as easily arouse or wound
even when unspoken, their mere thought can cause hope
or despair to enter your poor heart
cowardly lion behind your rib cage,
some words can put you to sleep
some words can make you weep,

some without warning can make you laugh out loud or stun
you into silence, deafen or
dumb you
their abracadabra can weave spells
change matter, make manna of it
it is as if words
were physical, which of course they are, sound waves,
they are not emotional, in themselves,
but I suspect they care
when they're uttered, the light rap of their

consonants, their vowels in place
their very spelling important to them, I feel sure
they have their morphology as
you do, they insist
behind closed doors, felt-lined,
on tilde and circumflex, that there is worth
in orthography and there is worth
in geography as well—for words, that is
words correctly spelled have, in truth,
destinations, their thud as if on peace, as if on cloth

is so quiet, so light the heart could turn to stone
from such unbearable lightness
only shamans can know the magic of weights
only shamans the exact order of letters in a name or a place,
how to spell them right
and when the words have flown
as if they were birds
or a child's kite with a tail on a string,
or when they float down
on air, they break all places intended and known

Stargazer

The very stars are justified.
The galaxy
italicized.

I have proofread
and proofread
the beautiful script.

There are no
errors.

Stefan

Stefan
aged eleven
looked at the baby and said
When he thinks it must be pure thought
because he hasn't any words yet
and we
proud parents
admiring friends
who had looked at the baby

looked at the baby again

Stories of Snow

Those in the vegetable rain retain
an area behind their sprouting eyes
held soft and rounded with the dream of snow
precious and reminiscent as those globes –
souvenir of some never nether land –
which hold their snowstorms circular, complete,
high in a tall and teakwood cabinet.

In countries where the leaves are large as hands
where flowers protrude their fleshy chins
and call their colours
an imaginary snowstorm sometimes falls
among the lilies.
And in the early morning one will waken
to think the glowing linen of his pillow
a northern drift, will find himself mistaken
and lie back weeping.
And there the story shifts from head to head,
of how, in Holland, from their feather beds
hunters arise and part the flakes and go
forth to the frozen lakes in search of swans –
the snow light falling white along their guns,
their breath in plumes.
While tethered in the wind like sleeping gulls
ice boats await the raising of their wings
to skim the electric ice at such a speed
they leap jet strips of naked water,
and how these flying, sailing hunters feel
air in their mouths as terrible as ether.
And on the story runs that even drinks
in that white landscape dare to be no colour;
how, flasked and water clear, the liquor slips
silver against the hunters' moving hips.
And of the swan in death these dreamers tell
of its last flight and how it falls, a plummet,

pierced by the freezing bullet
and how three feathers, loosened by the shot,
descend like snow upon it.
While hunters plunge their fingers in its down
deep as a drift, and dive their hands
up to the neck of the wrist
in that warm metamorphosis of snow
as gentle as the sort that woodsmen know
who, lost in the white circle, fall at last
and dream their way to death.

And stories of this kind are often told
in countries where great flowers bar the roads
with reds and blues which seal the route to snow –
as if, in telling, raconteurs unlock
the colour with its complement and go
through to the area behind the eyes
where silent, unrefractive whiteness lies.

Suddenly

A cock pheasant
broke cover   rose
from the chrysanthemums
as I bent to pick
the shaggy wet-petalled flowers
for a bowl
in my darkening house

rose
straight up from my feet
with such a whirr and roar
of his beautiful engines
that the flowers
fell from my hand
and the scissors
open-mouthed
froze

This Heavy Craft

The wax has melted
but the dream of flight
persists.
I, Icarus, though grounded
in my flesh
have one bright section in me
where a bird
night after starry night
while I'm asleep
unfolds its phantom wings
and practises.

This Sky

Tonight
beneath this sky
I could plunge my hands
in snow
and pull forth goldfish.

Traveller's Palm

Miraculously plaited tree.
A sailor's knot
rooted,
a growing fan
whose grooved and slanted branches
are aqueducts
end-stopped
for tropical rains.

Knot, fan,
Quixote's windmill,
what-you-will –
for me, traveller,
a well.

On a hot day I took
a sharp and pointed knife,
plunged,
and water gushed
to my cupped mouth

old water
tasting green,
of vegetation and dust,
old water, warm as tears.

And in that tasting,
taster, water, air,
in temperature identical
were so
intricately merged
a fabulous foreign bird
flew silent from a void

lodged in my boughs.

Truce

My enemy in a purple hat
looks suddenly like a plum
and I am dumb with wonder
at the thought
of feuding with a fruit.

Winter Morning

Had Van Gogh never lived
how could I have seen
as I switched on the light,
that Van Gogh-yellow room
and beyond it, his bright
delphinium blue
of dawn on the snow?

The World

It is like a treacle, the world.
I am caught in its golden threads,
a fly in a honey pot.

Young Girls

Nothing, not even fear of punishment
can stop the giggle in a girl.
Oh, mothers' trim
shapes on the chesterfield cannot dispel
their lolloping fatness.
Adolescence tumbles about in them
on the cinder schoolyard or behind the expensive gates.

See them in class like porpoises
with smiles and tears
loosed from the same subterranean faucet; some
find individual adventure in
the obtuse angle, some in a phrase
that leaps like a smaller fish from a sea of words.
But most, deep in their daze, dawdle and roll;
their little breasts like wounds beneath their clothes.

A shoal of them in a room makes it a pool.
How can one teacher keep the water out,
or, being adult, find the springs and taps
of their tempers and tortures?
Who, on a field filled with their female cries,
can reel them in on a line of words
or land them neatly in a net?
On the dry ground they goggle, flounder, flap.

Too much weeping in them and unfamiliar blood
has set them perilously afloat.
Not divers these – but as if the waters rose in flood
making them partially amphibious
and always drowning a little and hearing bells;
until the day the shoreline wavers less,
and caught and swung on the bright hooks of their sex,
earth becomes home – their natural element.

Zero Is Zero

(from *Alphabetical*)

I have circled zero
over and over
in love with the aperture
where the face of light
might appear.

With Euclid's compass
I draw beautiful circles.
I trace man-hole covers, ride Ferris wheels,
wear rings on my fingers –
all are zero.
A port-hole awaiting that luminous face.

How visualize nothingness –
rare gift from Arabia –
absence of all magnitude?

And – afterwards?

How anticipate
afterwards?

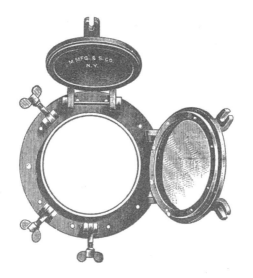

Previously Published Work

Poetry

As Ten as Twenty, 1946
The Metal and the Flower, 1954
Cry-Ararat! Poems New and Selected, 1967
P. K. Page: Poems Selected and New, 1974
Evening Dance of the Grey Flies, 1981
The Glass Air, 1985, 1991
Hologram: A Book of Glosas, 1994
The Hidden Room: Collected Poems (in two volumes), 1997
And Once More Saw the Stars: Four Poems for Two Voices
    (with Philip Stratford), 2001
Alphabetical / Cosmologies, 2001
Planet Earth, 2002
Hand Luggage: A Memoir in Verse, 2006

Poetry Anthology

To Say the Least: Canadian Poets from A to Z, (editor) 1979

Prose

The Sun and the Moon, 1944, 1973
Brazilian Journal, 1988
Unless the Eye Catch Fire, 1994
A Kind of Fiction, 2001
The Filled Pen: Selected Non-Fiction, 2006
Up On the Roof, 2007

For Children

A Flask of Sea Water, 1989
The Travelling Musicians, 1991
The Goat That Flew, 1994
A Grain of Sand, 2003
A Brazilian Alphabet, 2005
Jake, the Baker, Makes a Cake, 2008

About P. K. Page

P. K. Page was born November 23, 1916, at Swanage, Dorset, England. In 1919 she left England with her family who settled in Red Deer, Alberta. She went to school in Calgary and Winnipeg and in the early 1940s moved to Montreal where she worked as a filing clerk and researcher. She belonged to a group that founded the magazine *Preview* (1942–45) and was associated with F. R. Scott, Patrick Anderson, Bruce Raddick, Neufville Shaw and A. M. Klein. Her poetry was first published in *Unit of Five* (1944) along with that of Louis Dudek and Raymond Souster. From 1946 to 1950 Page worked for the National Film Board as a scriptwriter. In 1950 she married William Arthur Irwin and later studied art in Brazil and New York.

P. K. Page is the author of more than a dozen books, including poetry, a novel, short stories, essays and books for children. A memoir entitled *Brazilian Journal* is based on her extended stay in Brazil with her late husband who served as the Canadian Ambassador there from 1957 to 1959. A memoir in verse, *Hand Luggage*, explores in a poetic voice Page's life in society and in the arts.

Awarded a Governor General's Award for poetry (*The Metal and the Flower*) in 1954, Page was also on the short list for the Griffin Prize for Poetry (*Planet Earth*) in 2003 and awarded the BC Lieutenant Governor's Award for Literary Excellence in 2004. She has eight honorary degrees and is a Fellow of the Royal Society of Canada. She has also been appointed a Companion of the Order of Canada.

Painting under the name of P. K. Irwin she has mounted one-woman shows in Mexico and Canada and been exhibited in various group shows. Her work is represented in the permanent collections of the National Gallery of Canada, the Art Gallery of Ontario, the Victoria Art Gallery and many collections here and abroad.